THE BLISS IS IN THE STUMBLE

JEFFREY BRYAN GRUBERT 5/17/17

EDITED BY:

JUDYTH HILL

MICHELLE GRUBERT

PUBLISHED BY: SURRENDER TO WIN, INC.
2016

First Printing: 2014

Second Printing 2015
ISBN-13: 978-1-50-300660-7

Surrender To Win, Inc.
2661 West Noble Vista Dr.
Prescott, AZ 86305
949-929-8880

Ordering Information:

Special discounts are available on quantites for purchase. For details contact the publisher at the contact info above.

US trade bookstores and wholesales: Please contact Surrender To Win, Inc. at 949-929-8880.

*Mystery calls
to foreign ventures,
take note
of her direction,
prepare for full
disclosure.*

*For Michelle, Sophia Rose,
Lily Claire & Gianna Clementine*

&

Her invisible magnificence whose everlasting gift is bliss.

Acknowledgments

It has taken a year to write *The Bliss is in the Stumble* but a lifetime of experience with people along the way who have caught me, held me, let me go, guided and prayed for me along the way.

It is with deepest gratitude, I salute Bill Wilson and the thousands of men and women in "the rooms" who have helped me surrender to an incredible awakened life.

Special Thanks...

To Fr. Richard Rohr whose underlying themes in his teaching about the path of descent and transformation have helped me better understand and find the beauty and adventure in darkness, failure, relapse, death, and woundedness that shows up along the way. As he says, these have become my primary teachers, rather than ideas or doctrine. His teachings have blessed and confirmed my desire to wander in the wilderness for a season or two and helped me to reap the great blessings of a much larger conversation with the animate world.

To Bill Plotkin, friend and guide to soul, whose love has been as big as any wilderness we trekked this year and whose deep compassion has been the light on the path which helped me take the plunge into the wild mountain lakes of my psyche.

To Sheila Belanger, friend and guide to soul, who read my heart's desire in that special time and place and gave me permission to chase the storm. I've been writing about it every since.

To my editor Judyth Hill, who baptized me as poet on Valentine's Day 2014 in the lobby of the Hotel Real de Minas, San Miguel De Allende, Mexico. Who says we don't go to any length to find our voice?

To Katayo, Spirit Dancer, Underworld Scout, Sage Guide, Sacred Healer, Cocoon Weaver, Keystone, Kokanee, Silver Moon, Groundwater, Bone Women, Honey Badger Lover, Story Tender, Sacred Heart, thank you for your witness and love for Kingdom Dreamer, Poet & Slayer. You are all proof that heaven is on earth. I'm still singing about us!

To my mother Susanne Grubert, may she rest in peace. Her divine, invisible presence in the kingdom of birds was felt in the color of that wild place in May this year.

To my father, Gordon Grubert, whose unconditional support and love in my early years provided the freedom to make mistakes and find my path to soul.

Foreward

When I met Jeffrey Grubert in San Miguel de Allende, at the 2014 Writer's Conference, it was clear he was a man on divine fire. Poetry had lit him from inside: he had been Called.

Successful by every standard that we modern Americans tend to judge success, Jeff's meditation practices and passionate spiritual longings drove him to actively question and re-envision his life, and ultimately to give himself over to live his Soul's purpose.

The same inner work that led Jeffrey to follow his Soul's destiny, gifted him with a Call to Poem.

And with all his heart and spirit, he answered.

These poems mark the journey, the stepping stones, on his path.

Poetry requires of her devotees that we understand that our form demands more than just a message. Having something to say is not enough. Our urge to share what we think, believe, hope, dream, wonder, and know must marry a love of rhythm, and a profound loyalty to working inside the deep music of language.

As poets, we must dearly love and respect the Mystery, even as we delicately explore her enigmatic underpinnings. As the ones that make a sound resound in the world, we must, first and always, honor the Silence that rivers beneath all speaking.

In the months of gentle revision on these poems, Jeff gave himself unstintingly to the task of polishing his work, bringing the poems into a shining, unified whole.

And now this collection gleams! Message and medium merged!

In Jeff's poem, *Invisible Trust,* he says, "There is no life/ that satisfies a restless soul / except full surrender.....and in *The Bliss is in the Stumble,* Jeffrey has done exactly that: surrendered to the mysterious Call of his Soul, and to the holy Call of Poem.

Now it is your turn to have your heart lifted and your soul enlivened by this thoughtful and insightful collection, it was my pleasure to help birth.

Judyth Hill
October 29, 2014

Preface

Poet Mary Oliver writes, "Tell me, what is it you plan to do with your one wild and precious life?" In offering this book, I invite you to explore your one wild and precious life. In Genesis 1:27, we read about God saying, "Let us make humans in our image, according to our likeness." This is an invitation for you to explore that image - to engage in a larger conversation with the animate world and to reclaim your original voice without apology, shame or insecurity. It's your birthright to pursue this spiritual adventure, and you can choose that journey today. Beginning or continuing your unique sacred dance could lead you to discover truths about yourself that you were born to discover. I assure you the world needs your deepest self as much as you do. Bringing your true self to a broken world can ultimately contribute to the healing of the earth and all its inhabitants. It's an invitation to get back into "right relationship" with all living creatures, human and non-human. Your life is not about you and you may have a deeper calling just under the surface of your best made plans.

Into descent I slipped, a descent to soul. This was not a random act of surrender or an escape into the wilderness alone. This descent was with three guides and 12 other soul seekers. (www.animas.org) There have been thousands of surprises along the way, one of which is this book of poems. As a result of this plunge, I'm here to report there is life after death, but I had to do some dying first. A thousand time in this life I've been asked to die before my physical death. To die before I die. This path is not without danger, for there are parts of my ego that need to die. Protective parts that have kept me safe since childhood, but are now obstacle to living a happy, joyous and free life. These parts have had to die for me to take new risks and experience new adventures in the second half of life.

May these poems find a home in your imagination and fuel your desire to seek a place of soul in this world so you can find a path to serve the greater good and make a difference. Mystery (God) is calling. It's true, the destination may be unknown, but where Mystery (God) will take you is always good. With healthy direction, some structure, and a bit of discipline, the Universe will support your unique journey. It might be helpful to know that you have all the resources within yourself to navigate your unique grand adventure. It is my hope that you'll take the necessary time out of your busy life and explore the process of recovering and discovering the wonderful characteristics of your "one wild and precious life." The world desperately needs you.

Wild Blessings!

Jeffrey Bryan Grubert
Kingdom Dreamer, Poet, & Slayer

Table of Contents

Living Inside Out

It is a worthy cause
to seek the mysterious
ever changing face of God.

To lead our fellows
into great inner adventure
self-discovery
shadow dancing
wandering, letting go.

Imagine a purpose
that would not save
the world
as much as reconnect
ourselves
to the healing
power of Earth.

We need to rest now
put our work
back into perspective.
We need to turn off
our cell phones
stop escaping into
science fiction,

find adventure again
in the creek and canyons
in our own backyard.

I am climbing trees
chasing red hawks
pausing in awe
feeling hummingbirds
free dive
just inches above my head
leaving my entire being
humming, desiring
my own
supercharged flight.

Let's take a journey inside
for the greatest peace march
ever.

Let's do the real work
of living and dying
together.

Invisible Trust

Who am I
to attempt the impossible,
to stop and change direction
in the middle of my life?

Mystery has broken in
and rearranged the furniture
overnight

I have lost the magic
of my youth.
I am rewriting
the American dream.

It is my hope
my resistance
will be spit
from the belly of the whale
like Jonah.

There is no life
that satisfies a restless soul
except full surrender
of body and bones
to sacred Earth
in summer.

Shadowland

No action is a waste of time
but holding the wind
is impossible -
so stop trying.

If you remain
a kite on a string
the Master will never
lead you.

Follow your breath
Yahweh, Yahweh
hear the Creator
whisper you home.

There is an urgency
in silence
a power driving force
inviting you to spiritual adventure.

Plunge into shadows
that sprawl across
the rolling grass meadow
of your life, longing for birth.

Face your scars first
remember your losses
know that everything dies
then move on.

Be grateful for every encounter,
like a hawk
in full frontal dive
swiping fish from a majestic lake.

Return to enjoy the capture.
Be generous with your catch,
be clear on what you must devour.
Your soul longs to be your prey.

Exit Signs

Wanderers of wanderers
miracle of miracles,
mystery calls
I respond.

Canyon walls
like sandcastles
rise like protectors
for invisible guides

Warning me:
no human desires
upon this beach.

A minute's hike
from freeway spinning
the gift of this space
is impossible to grasp.

Winter's breath
is in the air
fall colors
light the dusk.

Fires in the sky
arrest the moment
from heart
to desire.

Even seagulls
have flown
off shore.

Alone on this beach
piles of stones
keep watch
for returning surf.

A fortress to hold
lover's secrets
who dare
slip it on for size.

The horizon
too vast to tumble,
only questions
answers to humble.

A guessing game
will rise and fall
the tides will wash
my tidy soul.

Baptized underwater
needlelike seaweed
electrifies my genitals

Below the skin
my circulation is circulating
I howl to the swirly moon
with Venus in her wake.

Decompose

What do I know of night?
I am not awake
my exhaustion washes away my dreams
the darkness is too vast to comprehend
the hours of night pass without permission.
Into descent I slip
in search of healing rest
God's forgiving hands at work
welcomes my Muse in dreams
softening the blow to my body.

I am rendered speechless
with a thousand questions
now obsolete,
my only desire is relief
from total suffocation.

Breathless
I am black and blue
running wild
like vinegar that strips the rust
from a corroded heart.

My last stance is weeping.
I face another night
alone, asleep, in expectation,
another awakening
in hope of knowing night.

Retreat

I have found
a cave
perched above
a path
cutting through
a canyon

Just out of sight
I have been swallowed
alive
Yet spared
to see an ancient
space

having mercy
on me
The afternoon sun
strips me
of all protection

Naked
my work addiction
is revealed
Yet I have not missed
"the" call

Playing hooky
with Winter brush
rolling in silky
sand dirt

like a kid on a beach
but inside a stone
on the side
of a canyon wall

I find myself
terribly alone
Come play with me
I cannot leave.

Shedding Insight

Turn away
from all I love
storms always pass
a blue sky returns
Montana's big sky
meets Clark Fork River
somewhere downstream
my gushing tears
wash away
ancient blues
and ancestor's wounds
I have carried
these pains
to this final day
I have wept above
the treelines
that hang in the balance
and walk to safety
at the edge
of my own destruction
the clouds
rise like smoke
from invisible
fire ceremonies
beneath the forest wall
from an intimate exchange
it's hard not to believe

I'm burning a hole in this page
my desire has turned elsewhere
now undiscovered
among seeds
planted this summer
close your eyes
picture this
a dying tree
giving birth
to a family
of honey bees
Sweet paradox sting!
Sweet paradox sing!

Sing

Sing
moonless sky,
black clouds are parting.
cracks of starlit spaces
peer through, gazing down.
Chosen by Mystery
to capture moments
of light and dark,
to wrap my twisted soul
around
a strategic mind
that honors time.
No imagination or romance
softens the prison walls
of the male mind.
The only love affair
with Her
that connects me to Earth
is Her.
I have ignored
Her steadfast, endless,
calling.
She pins me down
on Zendo floor
for praise and
mindful presence.

The childhood pain
lets go today
to dream with Her
in plenty.

Animate Mystic

There's a west trail
calling attention tonight,
it's got nothing to offer
but a alluring, blind path.

In the thicket
the crickets
announce every step
cleansing the air
with sweet reminders
we are alive tonight.

At river's edge
reflections reveal
a ripple effect
created by midnight
moon shadows
that float on the surface.

Evening dew drops drip
creating small passages
that no-see-um insects
can swim in.

Mystery swallows
us whole
when we peer
into the mirror of water.

Nothing doing.
No change.
Stagnation traps us
inside old boxes
of melting cardboard.

This place we live
drowning out
creativity, imagination
growth-making.

What is this success?
A failure to live?
The experiment
is expiring
without even trying.
How will we survive
without capital infusion
of creativity?

There's a thousand
online apps to download -
are we uploading our imagination
into cyberspace?

Are we drinking
plastic and silicon waste?
Breathing chemical haste
with our heads glued
to Iphones?

Lost in Facebook
a false sense of connection
seeking some unknown source
to restore our soul
again and again.

I need to get my hands off
the keyboard
and monitor the Milky-Way
in the concrete jungle.

I cannot see where I live.
I don't think people
in my neighborhood
are happy -
their smiles are pasted
to their reality
not on the dreams
they're missing.

Will I miss the boat too
or will I just keep smiling
about the one reality I know?

I have tasted freedom.
It's dark and lovely
leading me nowhere,
bringing me
face to face
with the challenge
of a brand new world.

Domesticated Escape

It's taken me all day
to get here,
both lost and found.

I've been muddling
all morning
in my thoughts
falling short
not living up.

I can't hike
far enough
I've packed
a heavy load,

clinging to
"too much stuff."
Lifting heavy gear,
beating myself up.

Next time
I desire
a lighter load
that won't pull
me down.

A tool
to help
cast away
old stories,
clear a path.

To cast
a stiff sail,
to catch
the wind.
To fly
to heaven.

There I go again,
away, away,
both lost and found.

Everyday Union

Morning silence stings
with expectation
begging me
for deliverance this year.

My open journal
draws my tears
telling a love story
that exposes the hole in my heart.

Amazed, I meet
the Master's indwelling
on Christmas Day
in a childlike way.

A burning desire
to grasp the unreachable
precious, earthly delights.
Tangible assets that slip
through my thoughts.

No place to hang my hat,
satisfy my hunger
devour dangerous landscape.
I'm left only with barren deserts.

In gratitude I receive
a promise of future relief
a relentless flash flood
that wash the images downstream.

Deep in the darkness
I'm led, hand in hand
to the edge of my desire
and asked to set the entire scene on fire
then walk away unharmed.

A moment of transformation,
an opportunity to love.
A mysterious connection
to the universal loneliness
of this moment.

Deserted

My heart is heating up.

The smell of old manure
rises from the path,

Google weather got it wrong,
the Southern sun is burning away the clouds.

My protection has vanished
but the cool ocean breeze remembers me.

Not much "wild" life here in late July:
signs warn of mountain lions,
but squirrels nest beneath the signs.

The old oak trees are panting
surrendering their dried out leaves
before their Fall time.

They are thirsty, the drought is winning.

Rumor has it a storm is lurking to the East -
even cumulus clouds are having second thoughts.

The heat is driving storms away,
any chance at helping Mother Earth
transform her dry skin is dashed.

I feel my skin burning now with hers.
It is clear,
eventually I will be completely exposed!

I am chasing storms
that head to dry deserted places of my soul.

There I thirst for mystery's kind embrace
to lead me across the sea of soil, sand
and fallen leaves.

My thirst is waiting to be quenched by my muse's hand
guiding me west toward the deep
Pacific blue.

Love Grieving

To think this moaning
would bring
such a morning.

Ecstatic relief -
bodily Incarnation
through *soulcraft*.

Pools of grief
bring forth
a wellspring.

I swim in dark
currents
with ancestral
ghosts

begging me to cast
deadly burdens
adrift.

My surrender
on desert floor
becomes my
lenten ashes.

For if I burn
with burdens thus
a new moon
is sure for rising.

I will take stance
awakened
sinking in
deep, wet sands,

to smell
chaparral and lavender
blooming.

Me in my wounding
you with your history
meet Earth in her
broken creation.

Together at last
basking in grief
to witness
the sun setting.

The nightfall
homecoming
starlight forthcoming
we melt
to climax.

I reflect now
the ending
I wish I had extended
the long-suffering
of the heavens.

To meet our embrace
with sacrifice
and grace.

It's Her heart
that devours
our grieving.

Inner Critic's Rest

I have hit a wall
run out of steam
my body is wrecked
I am forced to ask
for selfish desires

To stretch into this
new landscape
past my grief
my resistance
to utter surrender

Your abundant love
is my final exit strategy
everything bends
as all I care for
is your adoption

Kicking and screaming
everything I love
will be your inheritance
all will pass this way
no matter how I judge
how I cling
to some wrong idea
of you

Stumbling I am forced
to lay prostrate
before the gold
you lay at my feet

I see in the end
that there is more
darkness than light
to apprehend
I am your great
treasure jewel
waiting to be
plucked from your
refinery.

Like fire in your
holy kiln
you will burn
your desired image of me
on mystery's hands

So I, golden clay,
can emerge
a finished useful pot.

Synchronicity

Look here! These blankets
invite me to uncover
this garden and fall inside
the bright, blue Mexican sky.

To start living underground
in a paradise of paradox,
to find my soul
here and now.

This is the land of
St Michael the Archangel
whose goodness and power
are disguised as dragons.

I cry out to them
panting and screaming
praying to be devoured
by the fire in their belly.

Blessed breath of flame
turns to cooing doves
that guide my every step
morning, noon, and night
They lead me to still gardens
where hummingbirds confirm

that I was born to dance,
to sing of romance.
Something terribly lovely
happened on this holy ground,
I feel it in my bones.
I am, for the first time, haunted.

I need to know who is wooing me now.
Is it the same spirit that birthed me in 1962?
Born on the edge of the psychedelic movement
I am living the dream of a psychedelic life.

I live where Timothy Leary got high,
I write beyond the tracks where a beatnik died.
I have been gifted with a free pass
through the Summer of Love.

Allowed to die in winter's nest
and rise again in the Easter of mid-life,
I release my need for a purpose-driven life
to become a precious piece of *God* candy.

Cooked to sweet perfection,
sacrificed as someone else's treat.
Would this place be the same
if I had not found my soul here?

Shadows of wrinkled willow trunks
crawl to meet me on the ground
reminding me that everything will disappear tonight.
I have removed my shoes to honor the soon departure.

How could such a funeral of parting
be such insurance of a future encounter?
I will uphold the invitation to
move on and disappear.

We have done this
romantic dance
so many times
I've come to cherish it everyday.

The bliss is in this stumble.

Soul Encounter

Empty pages
same old stories
an international best selling
lie.

No real plot
no redemption of character
Read the book 10,000 times:
the day's as fresh as ever.

Years of study, work and hustle.
Words will fill the lonely page
like a dried-up well
with a broken bucket
or boarded-up school house
with weeping children.

My soul is patient
in disrepair.
She cannot breathe without
my writing,
She cannot speak without
my singing.
She prevails alone at
shadow boxing.

She hides out in malls
when people are shopping
when cars breakdown
or storms cause havoc.

Pride slips through the cracks
to recover the blunder
admit all your faults
and recover

Now you're prepared
for soul encounter.

Your Kingdom Come

There is only one you
you have only this one
precious life

You are here to recover
your soul image

To seek in the dark
walk into the face of fear

Discover the one you
are most in love with

The one that you have been
dissing for months, days and years
It's time for return, reclamation,
rewriting, crossing over, letting go
dying and resurrection.

It's time to greet
the one that longs for the
wild and wonderful life.

No one will claim you for their own
only you can claim you

Deep self-compassion
is the way
to love and care
for others,

The most authentic
way to serve

It's where your magician
king, lover and warrior live

Once you experience
your unique soul vision
your ego will learn to serve her

You will become "right sized,"
it's the dance she's been crying for

She is helpless without you
She has no hands or feet
on earth but yours.
She needs you to find her in the dark
then serve her during the day.

Please don't try to figure it out
or try and fix anything

Be your wild self
get naked with creation
follow her unending trail

Be in the moment
surrender to win
wander and let her guide you

Sooner and later
patience will mold you
the images will guide you

Your descent
will transform you

It will open the portal
for others to fall into

One by one
each soul will be reclaimed
by its birthright

The soul and the ego
will find rest in each other

Life and death
will be remembered as best friends

This is where peace
and fearlessness
meet and live forever

At the threshold
the center point
the jumping off place

The place we cannot deny
it's the beach where
Jonah was spit out of the sea
by the whale

It's the kingdom
on Earth place
where all souls lead the way

in perfect harmony
but all beating
to a different drum

A death march
that ends
in a glorious
public burial

Hear the applause
for the Wicked Witch
of the West in us
is dead.

We march into
the north
to weather
winter's storm

which always
births spring
summer
then a deeper fall

The spiral of life
deepens our faith
until we become
the Earth again.

All is complete
we live forever

Wheat and
weeds
caressing the
living experiment
together.

Ad Infinitum

Counting down hours
the final day
of the year
I move across dirt roads
to canyon silence
meeting a monastic library
filled with
nurturing wild words
pronounced
from basements
of ancient world religions.

Throw in a few books
on time travel
and transcendental meditation -
Are all methods of shape-shifting
right?

Overwhelmed by words
collecting dust on the shelf
I make my way to
the round building of prayer

inside the floor drops
like an underground cavern
reminding me of ancient
kivas restored at the
Canyon of the Ancients
in Cortez, Colorado.

How can I take any position
of knowing anything
when so many men and women
throughout the ages
have taken every possible
position of knowing something
that I have no time to learn?

I was sure my path
lonely
I was sure my path
unique
I wake up
honoring fellow pilgrims
on my way to the monastery.

At the threshold
of prayer
I am greeted
by a young monk
protecting the cave of wisdom
I win his trust
by removing
my dirty socks
then step down.

Barefoot I walk
on sweat stained carpets
where people have prayed
on knee and ass
for 100 years.

It seems others have been
hungry throughout the ages,
hunting wild beasts from within
while chasing honeybees
who pursue to sting
their soul.

Millions of people
on flat land below
are moving to and fro,
I am on retreat
hoping to never
return the same.

I am attempting
a metamorphosis
in plain sight.

A change in character
discipline and vocation
that requires
night vision like a
patient old owl
who watches
my shadows crawl
across the zendo floor

All thoughts
become strangers
in the night
passing now in daylight
safe to compare
my addictions to theirs
for this awareness
we share as crucifixion.

Transparent
and vulnerable
I am safe for viewing
people have never really
seen me anyway.

It's their misconception
of me
that I am disappearing from.

This experiment
is unproven
and may be
a ridiculous
self-sabotaging act
that unites
us in my anxiety
of being wrong.

Can we find confirmation
and communion
in that?

I have finally arrived
at the wrong time
for prayer
apologizing to monks
for tracking dirt
in the temple.

The most important scripture
I uncover
on this new years day
is that I am here
ready to have
the conversation
I've been preparing to have
since I was born.

Waking

See the silvery light of the moon
track the space between the cells of our souls
and the stars scattered against the dark morning sky.

Coyotes howl from the East
to warn of the advancing sunrise
that aims to blind our night vision
chasing the dream-maker to dreaming.

Cottonwood companions take morning drink
from river waters running below,
where yesterday
we submerged an abundant life
we loved living

Like liquid acid, the water dissolves the need to know
sends the senses weeping.
This death trip downstream,
a return, a rest,
a birthing bath for our imagination.

The new day's sun
sets cold canyons on fire
wakes us from our mourning.

At river's edge we die to cross,
to capture the one true life,
we've longed to save from drowning.

Grief calls out.

We will meet downstream,
where winter meets spring,
where surprised we find,
we've been together all along.

Secretly dancing,
in the silvery light of the moon,
which has guided us to this
new magnificent morning.

Stone Works

Use canyon stone
for red rock sculptures.

Follow the flaws,
run your vision
through the gaps.

Close your eyes.
Feel your life flow
through the stone.

Winds cut,
remove the stubborn parts
of who you are.

Lead the way -
take chisel to core
in real hard matters:

expression, laughter
friendship, forgiveness.

The stone is softer
than it looks,
it's worth mounting
when the carve is over.

Let the work own you.
When the Master's complete,
it's His perfection.

The stone
is yours to keep,
to carry on your back
until tired.

Return it to the earth.
Bury it with your desire.
This becomes the headstone,
not you.

Mandorla

I have removed my clothes.

I'm playing dead
on a red table rock
rising high above
a Colorado canyon mesa
enacting a pure white
innocent human sacrifice.

The heat of the mid-day sun
softens my belly
the cool moisture of the stone
insures my back side is basted
ready for pressure cooking.

Hot and cold
scream for my affection.
Neither win -
both transform.
The tension of opposites
preserves me in perfect limbo.

The sky above speaks to my sacred heart:

What are you afraid of?
Why are you running
all the time?

I am waiting for simple answers
that never come,
the comfort of black and white thoughts
turn to a thousand shades of grey.

I become a cold cadaver
who cannot run from death.

My precious wild mind screams,
"What a treasured waste of time!"

I rise to live the rest of my life
between the rocky feeling of death
and what being alive is all about.

Wonder Runs Through It

At the edge
watching, listening
my heart ablaze, burning,
wonder runs through it.

Like a rigid rock formation
dangling on the side
of a treacherous mountain trail
somehow, my heart clings
to a tiny space

that keeps it from dropping
ten thousand feet below
to a running, rapid river
flowing to some unknown, unseen
mountain lake.

where water finds rest
in dancing sunlight
rays of hope
which tames the violent dream
freezing the flames
that would burn a hole in my heart.

So wonder can run through it again.

Late Bloomer

First to be last.
It's just that not all roads are straight.

There are alluring places
along the way
dark holes to be explored
to get lost in.

There is finding the way
through dead ends and poison ivy.
Meeting the tribe at the portal
we need to descend together.

Mystery is not an alone escape:
it's a community effort
discovering the care for the earth
grounding the Milky Way
in our collective imagination
underground.

It's not that I'm late.
I'm the missing piece
in a puzzle
desiring to complete
the desert scene
we dance in.

Passover

Even though I don't want to,
I have to say goodbye.

It doesn't make much sense
after all,
the party hasn't even started.

Goodbye to control
goodbye to leadership
the oldfashioned way.

Goodbye to my little girls
who don't need daddy anymore.
May they know God!!!

Goodbye to a wish, a prayer
a hope, a handful of suffering
goodbye to pushing away,
to dark and lonely journeys.

Goodbye to death
my deepest sympathy.

Aging Beauty

I am drifting downstream
like a twisted twig
used by children
to cook s'mores
on a fire
then tossed into a river
of sweet, sweet, despair.

Gentle summer running waters
reflect young pine trees
bending in the breeze
sweeping away
the safe sandy shores
I pray on.

The obsidian stone
scattered and broken
on shoreline
meets my prayer
and surrenders her blackness
to the soft nature of her being.

I greet her in child's pose
allowing me to feel
the tears that expose
the joy I've held for ransom.

I arise longing to see
through a new set of spectacles
with lenses of paradox
that remove judgment and shame.

Where my soul demands
higher dives
into deeper rapids,
wellsprings
with merciful encounters
that return holding
everything extraordinary.

Wild West

There is much to discover in the wild, Wild West
the veil is thin in the morning
A threshold between that jumping off place
and that march into a day of winning.

What would happen if we fell into a canyon of the west,
bounced along the red rock walls
broke all our old bones
landed on top of our shadows?

Like magicians in the fall,
let's spin into a beautiful, bloody, red dance,
so wild ones can catch their morning spirits,
span wisdom for the day.

Let's greet this day with openness,
like an unfolding, emerging butterfly,
soaring colorful sparks into the sky.

Who will speak for Her today?
Which portal will she descend?
Let's wed the broken parts and co-create,

making love in the morning.

My Word

There is a place of longing
in the deep
dark woods.

Only small rays of sunlight can penetrate.

A dance is pledged,
light piercing,
in wooded landscapes.
The wild, kind hands of winter hold.

Cold wars lurk behind the fall
which still hold
the hope
of summer's past.

Soon spring
will follow winter's clutching fist,
as sure as the seasons give and take
each other,
as fast friends.

We meet on our knees,
time and time again,
like lovers embracing,
transforming longing into truth.

I pledge a promise
for change.
My will becomes a rebel,
I cannot let go.

Grief never fails,
I'm a magician at a wellspring.
Changing reflections confirm,
life is not about me.

How anything changes, is real mystery to me.

I have found my part,
my inner peace,
in small rays of light
that sneak in between
my sleeping and waking.

Mystery takes me serious,
at my word.

Prayers of my heart,
hold me accountable
until I die.

Regrets on Death

I step into paintings
of childhood drama,
where innocent games
shift to heartbreak tears
and force the roles I play in.

Backyard swings
and forts in trees
were soul-centered
kingdoms to dream in.

Birds swirl high
to serve the play:
the flying,
a hard act to follow.

My final scene,
a dramatic death.

I pierce my heart in wonder.

Red raspberry jam,
sweet blood for effect,
is insurance for
standing ovation.

As childhood ends,
stepping down offstage,
the theatre opens up
in my bedroom.

I pause now, older,
to awaken in grief.
I've gone on without
real recognition.

By the choices I've made
to fit in and observe,
I've become an art collector.

In return for my joy
I bought all the art.
I pawned all my years,
making money.

I hung them on walls
to showcase my wealth
but I've become a
bankrupt spectator.

In my will,
I'm directing the show:
leave all the pictures
hanging.

Look real close
between brush strokes
and smudges
you can see the images
dancing.

A child holding hands
with a blindfolded monkey,
two butterflies soaring
for the heavens.

Wild willow trees bend
to touch an old man snoring
a blonde woman observing
his napping.

With one breast exposed
she offers her nursing
her right hand
held straight out
for stopping.

Curiosity calling
I step into the picture
despite her strange warning
scream.

Her gentle embrace
settles my soul to rest
I crossover and wake
as a masterpiece.

Breaking Addictions

We are withdrawing east
to face the north of our lives
to wander uncharted terrain
and meet our souls.

The adjectives are few
to describe
the beauty and the beast
within.

It's hopeless
extracting
"right words"
from our head,

our hearts are dying
to be discovered.
We face descent

for the rest of our life:
we can only seek
that which we do not know.

The seasons become one
rotating
experience, an endless embrace
sending us into a deeper trance
with the love
that created this space.

We have no place else to go.
Our wandering
has brought us home
to every sight
every sound
every moment
of our life.

Get up
get going
leave your little plans
and designs
for grander schemes
where your imagination
runs wild
on ancient mountain climbs
that melt
into limitless blue skies.

Follow red birds
overhead
who uncover seeds of hope
in spring.
Imagine what surprises
new birth can bring.

Feel the potential peril
let it sweep you away
on cloud rides
through troubled days.

Let fallen leaves
make puffy beds
for children's heads
to dream in.

Sit still,
while spinning
wild minds
bring you utter joy.

You see,
our wandering
has brought us home
to a place where our
soul can sing.

Where the setting sun
turns red rock glowing
on Colorado mesas.

Where wild mountain ponds
become pools of danger,
and the only response is,
"Jump in."

When miracle of flight
calls us to ride
soaring hawk
whose wingspan blends
with mountain views
and we forget
we cannot fly.

When evening breeze
guides season's passing,
and the hollows of October
bring soul-centered ghosts
to haunt empty
campfire benches
remembering the great
fellowship of Earth and Sky
together.

The stories still stand
like grass blades in sand
that surround
the once hot
fire pit.

They hold the space
which welcomes grace
where our souls
can sing forever.

Tracing Threads

Inspired by Emerson and Thoreau
as a kid
in a wilderness of dreams
coming true

wonderful rolling rides
to Half Moon Bay
fish and chips at roadside café
playing dead on sand dunes
near Carmel by the Sea.

Fogged in
on the streets of San Francisco
chasing hippie ghosts
at Haight and Ashbury

Tuning in new wave
as a punk rock poser
watching weeks of rainfall
fill the creek in my backyard.

Building cardboard boats
never failing to float
feeling the adrenaline rush
when the ship finally sinks

Hunting banana slugs
to see if they would burn
they do
using a whole book of matches.

Something torturing me
under my skin
testing my power
playing God
the taker of life
because of my lack of power
to create life.

I've met my shame and guilt
in wounded banana slugs
on Sunday morning slaughter
I return to it again and again
until I wake up in rehab.

I've made my amends
chasing rainbows now
at river's bend

I'm in
the second half of life
longing to hop in rapids
moving downstream
where the river will merge
into a spacious encounter
with an ocean of elders
who have thrown in
their white towels
of surrender.

Free to explore
empty space between the trees
protecting the shore
where the light of day
comes through to celebrate
the eternal welcome
of coming home.

Glorieta

I cherish this morning
humming with a thousand birds
swirling overhead

Crystal agate gardens glow
I follow the grey crooked lines
in their ancient peach colored forms.

A confederate army
was slaughtered here
bloodied souls bless this ground

I've fallen in the center
of a solid new universe
where wind and rain

glide in the tails of lightning strikes
restoring my strength
to welcome cosmic encounter

I feel the electric summer sky
with the railroad cars going by
In my stillness, see me fly.

The Awakened Path

I have been born anew
as a wild man
willing to wander with passion
into the heart of what it means
to belong to the earth
at this place and time in history.

I have accepted
with deep, deep, gratitude
the places of rest
that are being provided for my journey
and the willingness
to extend hospitality
to other wanderers on the path.

I desire to write my gospel
glorifying the Cosmic Christ
in actions worthy of words
which provide guidance
and strength
to cut my day world threads
that keep me from
the underworld journey.

May the gifts I bear
bring a warm light of comfort
to those who are still
afraid of the dark.

May my journey
and the stories I tell
be an open invitation
to those who may want
to venture into the dark.

May the Cosmic Christ
as manifested in my
four facets of self
be inner guides
To find my true self
in my second adulthood.

I've been given the wisdom
to feel
what season I am standing in
and what seasons are coming
and I welcome all storms
that divide and conquer
my need to be wrapped
in garments made of
safety pins and Elmer's glue.

May a community rise up
around me in this work
so that we may become a new culture,
beacons of hope
to the next generations.

Oh, land on fire
with no flames,

send your smoke signs
to cleanse our vision.

Be our guide to
new landscapes
that provide
the courage
to remove
old dwellings
and treasures
that have lost
their meaning.

You provide a perfect place
right here in our own backyard
to gather as priestly vessels
to encourage self-restraint
and overcome greed,
to stop the excuses
that waste our days
and rob our time
from soul ventures.

So, together,
in surrender,
let's keep the edges hot
inviting the shadows
to rest in the light.

28978139R00048

Made in the USA
San Bernardino, CA
12 January 2016